RAGGED EDEN

Michael Meyerhofer

GLASS LYRE PRESS

Copyright © 2019 Michael Meyerhofer
Paperback ISBN: 978-1-941783-58-0

All rights reserved: except for the purpose of quoting brief passages for review, no part of this book may be reproduced or transmitted in any form or by any means, electronic or mechanical, including photocopying, recording, or by any information storage and retrieval system, without permission in writing from the publisher.

Design & Layout: Steven Asmussen
Cover Art: © Dreamstime.com
Copyediting: Linda E. Kim

Glass Lyre Press, LLC
P.O. Box 2693
Glenview, IL 60025
www.GlassLyrePress.com

Ragged Eden

Acknowledgments

2River View — "The Animal Morgue," "On the History Channel's Lack of Imagination"

African American Review — "An Apology to Thin Air"

American Journal of Poetry — "Divine Witness," "Ode to Silhouettes," "Patriotic Cookie"

Arabesques Review — "Algebra Taught Me Nothing," "The Man with Six Hands"

Diode Poetry Quarterly — "The First Musician"

FRiGG — "After the Election," "New Year's Eve, 2016," "Literacy", "Why Don't You Dry Off After You Shower?" and "Flight Safety Instructions"

Moon City Review — "Adjunct," "The Dying Breed"

Open: A Journal of Arts & Letters — "Phantom Head Syndrome"

Permafrost Magazine — "Driving to the Airport"

Ragazine — "Piss-Poor," "When I was a Kid, So Many Died"

Southern Poetry Review — "Eighth Grade," "Truck Stop Lamentation"

South Dakota Review — "Women in the Bible had Pretty Eyes"

Split Lip — "The Conversationalist"

storySouth — "From the Hospital Bed"

Valparaiso Poetry Review — "The First Law of Thermodynamics"

Contents

Acknowledgments — v

I.

New Year's Eve, 2016	1
After The Election	2
Respawn	3
Ode to Silhouettes	4
An Apology to Thin Air	5
Portrait of a Child Tying His Shoe	6
The First Orphans	7
Truck Stop Lamentation	8
The Conversationalist	9
Tourists	10
Adjunct	11
Extinction	12
Falling Pianos	13
Divine Witness	14
Women in the Bible Had Pretty Eyes	15
And None of It Weighs A Thing	16
Literacy	18

Piss-Poor	19
Phantom Head Syndrome	20
Driving to the Airport	21
From the Hospital Bed	22
Fifteen Years After Not Much Happened	23
The First Musician	24

II.

Janus	27
The Bodhisattva Of Olive Avenue	28
The Shapeshifting Secret Agent Gets Caught Discarding A Sweater Knitted By His Girlfriend	29
The Dying Breed	30
The Man with Six Hands	31
The Animal Morgue	32
The First Law of Thermodynamics	33
Why Don't You Dry Off After You Shower?	34
Stoplight	35
Patriotic Cookie	36
Flight Safety Instructions	37
Maybe	38
Part Time Job	39
The Next Generation of Poets	40
The Lowest Wall in Human History	41

III.

The Great Speech	45
When I Was a Kid, So Many Died	46
On The History Channel's Lack Of Imagination	47
Machismo	48
Jack Dreams Of Attics And Snowfall	49
Not-God, Standing on the Beach, Talking to Herself	50

Ode to the Getaway	51
The Man Who Rises	52
Eighth Grade	53
Algebra Taught Me Nothing	54
My Mother's Left Eye	55
Dear Jung	56
Written at an Outdoor Café After News of Another American Killed in Battle at Afghanistan	57
On the Matter of Syrian Refugees, or Poem Written In The Seventy-Eight Year In Which We Haven't Learned A Thing	58
Upon Hearing that the Ringling Brothers Circus Is Closing Down After 146 Years	60
How to Be a Good Buddhist	61
Too Late	62
Ode to Nothingness	63
About the Author	65

Ode to the Getaway	51
The Man Who Rises	52
Eighth Grade	53
Algebra Taught Me Nothing	54
My Mother's Left Eye	55
Dear Jung	56
Written at an Outdoor Café After News of Another American Killed in Battle at Afghanistan	57
On the Matter of Syrian Refugees, or Poem Written In The Seventy-Eight Year In Which We Haven't Learned A Thing	58
Upon Hearing that the Ringling Brothers Circus Is Closing Down After 146 Years	60
How to Be a Good Buddhist	61
Too Late	62
Ode to Nothingness	63
About the Author	65

clearly I'm not needed,
yet I feel myself turning
into something of inexplicable value.

—*Mary Oliver*

It is possible to be brave.

—*Bin Ramke*

I.

New Year's Eve, 2016

That was the year nobody died:
all the musicians and actors,

the boxer, the poets, the Holocaust survivor,
an uncle in a star-spangled top hat,

their illnesses mere rumor
or at worst a reminder of something,

like a shawl thrown past the full moon.
And when, midway through winter,

the time came for reminiscence
and countdowns and champagne,

hardly anyone could think
of a single thing that had gone wrong,

which was itself quite unsettling.
So after a while, we gave up

trying to be sad and simply kissed
as the snows fell, transforming a nation

of lawns into canvases for trees
to scrawl their warnings in shadow.

After The Election

I'm having a hard time believing
we have so little iron in our blood

even in times of war, even after
the fifth or sixth heartbreak,

but the television documentary
insists each of us carries just enough

to make one sixpenny nail—
adequate to hang a college degree,

I suppose, but not Christ.
So that later, at the hardware store,

picking up a handful, I realize
I am holding a whole city block:

former classmates, dead relatives,
and a smattering of past lovers

who still prick my brain's fingers
when I try to squeeze them close.

Respawn

Maybe it's time I made some changes
thinks the goon with a machine gun

right before I rappel down behind him,
swinging my climbing gear like a hatchet.

I'm not sure I believe in this cause anymore,
grumbles the orc just as I release

the bowstring, the poison blow-dart,
the crackling death-spell.

Even the one-eyed dictator
pouring over casualty reports

wonders if he should finally give
representational government a chance

as my sniper scope inches
up his arm, a weightless insect

in a world where steel reflects fire
and death is a knot that unties itself.

Ode to Silhouettes

I mean those people who walk by
the camera, the movie screen, the stage

in a concert hall or a nightclub, so that
all you can see is their heads

and maybe a shoulder, slumped
or jerking a bit as they stumble free

of their row, untethered from their table
with its dark mysterious drinks,

on their way to the restroom
or the snack bar or the sidewalk

to return a call in spite of the rain.
So that whatever earrings they chose

become as meaningless as their hairstyle,
the effort put into matching

this blazer with that pair of shoes,
all of it backlit into passing obstruction,

the way sun-worshippers must still
groan or curse or at least take it

personally whenever the fat full moon
photobombs their view of God.

An Apology to Thin Air

When I stepped outside my house, I grimaced
because of how June roiled off the sidewalk,

wrinkling the porch-pose of my wife's orchids
and the sleek dark fur of the stray cat

lying in the shade of a planter, then I realized
my grimace just so happened to line up

with an old black man crossing the street,
and he frowned back at me, so that I stood there

unsure what to do next—if I should run
after him and explain the misunderstanding

or if that would only make matters worse;
besides, maybe he only looked that way

because of the awful heat which by then
had lasted so long, even the sprinklers

couldn't resuscitate those sad yellow lawns
lining our block in crisp, identical rows.

Portrait of a Child Tying His Shoe

Plato said children carry all knowledge inside them
and simply need the right impulse to wake it up,

the way we carry the raw antibodies to dead plagues
in the dank recesses of our genes, just in case.

John Locke described them as a *tabula rasa*,
their margins best filled in by flattery and praise.

And how often have we heard it said by now
that children learn languages better than we do,

a kind of communal, post-Babel consolation prize?
Still, when the farm boy knocks one to left field,

so far out that the catcher has nothing to do
but stoop, toss his glove, and garrote his shoelaces,

you can see it: there, beyond his fuming pantomime
of masculinity, the grace of his fingers dancing

a spell so profound, it takes two eyes, two hands,
and a choir of dendrites crackling in unison.

The First Orphans

She said, *I think this is called being naked.*
The boy didn't know what that meant

but it seemed kind of scary so he
sewed them skirts made out of fig leaves,

snaking grapevines around their kneecaps.
Then, for the first time, he noticed

the unashamed flexing of her toes
as she loitered by the trees. So he knelt

before a wild, as-yet-unnamed bush
and started braiding its thorns

into sandals. *Try these on.* She winced,
took a step, fell. He helped her up.

She decided not to hurt his feelings
so off they went. Before long, he got used

to her limping—she, to bleeding.
And everything kind of went from there.

Truck Stop Lamentation

They're saying goodbye to Lynette. Someone
has propped a blown-up picture on the bar,

a pixelated 50-something with bombastic hair,
and every once in a while, Lynette's friends

heft their steins to this makeshift grotto
or press lips to its glossy finish, never minding

who's been there before. I wonder if Lynette
would be flattered by all this attention:

throngs of chain-smoking women, unshaven
men in tank tops, one guy who walks out

of the restroom with a plunger over his crotch,
thrusting his way across the dance floor

to hymns of wild applause. I'm staying
at the motel across the street, just stopped in

for a quick beer, but they tell me that's fine,
Lynette would want me to stick around. A few

hug me despite my jacket and loosened tie.
Later, when I offer to pay for what I've drunk,

an old guy who hasn't said a word all night
looks up from a heap of peanut shells, his eyes

like two wet sharpened stones, and tells me
to put my damn wallet away. And I do.

The Conversationalist

I'm no good at talking to people
but I'm even worse talking to animals.

Whales roll their eyes, giraffes
cock their heads like prom queens,

my mere approach causes
the most patient platypus to dive

headlong into the gurgling stream.
Sadly, that's just the beginning.

Try as I might, I'm still the guy
whose chatter pissed off the Pleiades.

Mountains rebuff my small talk.
Even shadows dodge me at parties.

God, if only I hadn't learned to talk
by wasting hours at the window,

my good ear pressed to the glass,
listening to the stammer of rain.

Tourists

A bald monk met us at the door,
asked us what we were doing there.

I told him I only wanted to see
the inside of that bamboo pagoda,

charmed as we were driving
by its gated blossoms, the way

those jade and tangerine tapestries
hung between two knots

of traffic, straight as Shaolin arrows
despite the squeal of brakes

and the rumbling jag of rap music.
He made us take our shoes off.

I recognized the Li Po he recited,
though I've only read it in translation.

We went out to the gardens,
snapped a few pictures, then retired

to the red brick path leading back
to our rental car. At the last moment,

I looked up and saw a child
pressing her face to the glass,

her breath forming a white sunburst,
a toy airplane waving in her fist.

Adjunct

All my friends are buying houses
and rings that won't lime your fingers,

sometimes making the tough choice
between Italy and Amsterdam,

swapping war stories of committees
and escalating taxes and all

I have to share is my concern
that the sink will go dry

before I can rinse off the shaving cream,
and all I know is that their houses

grew from wood that grew over
the graves of prehistoric birds and gold

comes exclusively from the hearts
of supernovas—which makes them

smile since everybody loves
to hear what they already know.

Extinction

We woke to hear that all the world's zebras had begun
to shrink. By nine, they'd become the size of basset hounds.

Tadpoles by noon, dust by five. Scientists were baffled.
By midnight, zebras dwarfed the cells of lions, the mitochondria

of butterflies. Next morning, they simply drifted off
the lenses of microscopes like party balloons,

grazing on air. *They don't seem to be in pain,* said a man
in a long white coat, *just a bit sleepy.* By week's end,

we remembered how to yawn. Storefronts returned
to mannequins and smartphones. Even the hyenas forgot.

Though some nights, I swear I feel those zebras
floating upward on pillows of dark matter

like I am the penitentiary that fed them,
like ours was the ragged Eden they outgrew.

Falling Pianos

Implausible as the flying guillotine,
set up for politically incorrect

cartoons drawn by grandfathers,
still they draw us in, especially

on moving day: so many writers
congregating like pigeons

at the bottom of stairwells,
along sidewalks, below windows,

all of us looking up in time
to be paralyzed by that curse

followed by a heavy scrape of oak,
the music of vibrating teeth.

Divine Witness

It all started with Christ, you know.
So many dust-covered followers

passing bread, pouring wine
like whale's blood, when suddenly

the son of God whipped out his iPhone
and took a selfie. *Just sharing*

a snapshot of our meal, Christ said
when they asked what he was doing,

and for the rest of the evening
as he spoke of nails, and roosters,

and swords bought for the price
of a cloak, they listened

mostly to his breast pocket:
that steady, unanswered buzz.

Women in the Bible Had Pretty Eyes

Take that with a grain of Lot's wife.
Think of pebbles buried by rushing water,

sprinklers in a California drought,
bits of moon-black hair

missed by the skinning knife
still clinging to the cave-mouth,

whatever flesh keeps the rain out. God,
the sharpest blades are thin

as fingernails, break if bent. But women
in the Bible had eyes like porn stars,

like cattle: grass-fed, roving,
smarter than you think, smarter

than you think.

And None of It Weighs A Thing

Let's say you get a box in the mail,
the return address washed clean by rain.

Inside the box lies another box,
and so on. Most are just cardboard

but some are colored glass, plastic,
mahogany. Now and then you find one

sealed, its tight little lock just begging
for jailbreak. Others rest in ribbons

soft as calfskin or yawn half-open
like miniature grand pianos. You keep

opening. Before long, your labors
call for a jeweler's hammer and scope,

tweezers, nanites. You wonder
if such Russian intricacy suggests

a designer or if it's simply in the nature
of boxes to hold one another. Atoms

become down-quarks, tiny strings
of vibrating generosity. And so on

until both your imagination and your
toolbox lie exhausted. You curse.

Then you start backwards, stacking
each box in the one that came before.

When you're done, you tape that first
and final box shut, so that it looks

pretty much the same as it did
when you started. You raise it all

to your ear, you lift it like an infant
or an atom bomb. You shake it.

Literacy

I was terrified of pronouncing shirt
as shit, rap as rape, and most of all, beast

as breast, having already seen what happened
to those who committed such wrongs

in a world where just one letter separates
laughter from slaughter, when the sole way

to avoid ending up like a rain-whipped
sapling under thunderheads of grade school

ridicule was to worship the difference
between rectal and recital, to mouth

each syllable like a prayer—dust to dust,
firehose to firehouse, astray to ashtray.

Piss-Poor

How that adjective hung over our daily lives
like a loop of errand mistletoe, year long

those two glib syllables enough to distinguish
between regular Iowa-poor and those failed

dirt farmers down the road whose kids
seemed to know a bit too much about sex,

so poor that all they had was their own
personal spurt of the divine, which turns out

to be you, just you, handed back with the best
parts already spent on God knows what,

the remaining broth so heavy and gilded
that holding it, of course you feel like a king.

Phantom Head Syndrome

Everyone's talking about the latest kid
made to kneel in the desert so some guy

with a machete can cut his head off,
maybe the tenth such video looping across

the dark ether, and I remember volunteering
for a group that tracked kiddie porn sites

and reported them to the FBI. You can
imagine the result, like Holocaust footage

viewed so many times you hardly flinch
when bulldozers roll past the camera

whisking a pile of heads into a hole.
Talking to another volunteer, this ex-cop

on his umpteenth marriage, I said
the hardest thing for me was the lack

of closure, never knowing who if anyone
makes it out of that human sand trap.

Nah, he said, *the worst thing is
sometimes, the damn kids are smiling.*

Driving to the Airport

The last time I saw you, Mitchell County
dawn was just gilding the powerlines,

broad swaths of darkness between windmills.
Frost eased across the windshield, ghostly

palmprints. When you switched on the heater,
the vents rattled so badly you confessed

that a mouse must have crawled in and died.
We were literally hearing its bones quiver

like seeds in a popcorn maker. *Don't worry,*
you said. *It doesn't stink anymore.* I took

a breath, said you're right. *Of course I am,*
you laughed. *I pilot this wreck every day.*

From the Hospital Bed

I'm lying here reading story after story
about Zen masters precisely foretelling

the date and time of their own demise
when I remember my grandfather

who must have told us half
a hundred times that he'd be dead

by the end of the year then went on
living another two decades,

until his speech slowed and he
no longer cursed the length of skirts

on television or blamed his arthritis
on the Japanese, actually stopped

threatening to cut off his own legs
when rain rattled the eaves,

and mostly just wandered around
the house finally unattached

to the bottles of cheap beer
that had for so long sustained him

though he still stopped sometimes
to ask for a dish of ice cream.

Fifteen Years After Not Much Happened

I'm thinking about that night
second year in grad school

when we sat around and got blind
drunk on minimum wage wine

and you told me you were in love
with that poet in a wheelchair

but you were worried
because his last girlfriend

was flat-chested and you were
a triple-D and I told you

not to worry but you still lifted
your Flaming Lips shirt

like I was a doctor
you'd known all your life

and asked what I thought of them
so I repeated my prognosis

and stared until you said thanks
and refilled my cup the wine

blushing for both of us
as we switched to talking shop

so-and-so with the bad line breaks
sitting as close as friends do

having already touched
deeper than bones or blood.

The First Musician

Sometimes, I like to think about the first caveman
who invented the flute, how he must have

been out hunting something big and dangerous
one day when something caught his eye—

just some reeds sticking out of a pond, all muddy,
but for some reason he snapped one off,

shaped his breath through the opening
and heard it come out clean on the other side,

only changed somehow, more high pitched,
untamed, so that he thought about the wild cry

his child made when she entered the world,
slick as a fish, and as he carried that simple reed

back to the rest of his clan, carried it back
with the same hands that had thrown spears

through hides and ripped meat right off the bone,
he had to stop sometimes to rub his eyes.

II.

Janus

I've built a wall
between the two continents
of my brain, in the space
where I caught them
rubbing up against each other
like teenagers at a school dance.
On one side, God
knows why, I painted
a red barn leaning off a hill,
dappled in sea-light.
The other side?
For a while, I covered it
with spikes and razor wire
but I took them away
once I realized
they might be mistaken
for handholds.

The Bodhisattva Of Olive Avenue

A guy walks into the gas station
with one of those overcoats that says
he means to rob the place,
only there's an old radio
bandaged in duct tape hanging
from his sun-burnt neck,
blasting God-knows-what
as he spins and jives
between sales on wiper blades
and transmission fluid,
the speakers so worn the notes
might as well be pinballing off tin walls.
So that everybody looks up
from those tiered aisles of candy
and beef jerky and even the cashier,
who appears stoned beyond words,
starts this vaguely sexual
wriggle-dance which makes
the man with the stereo applaud
and cry, "Go on, man, express yourself!"
then turn and eye the rest of us,
his gaze both desperate and hopeful,
like he's about to start
some kind of movement. Only it doesn't
quite catch on, the cashier
stops dancing and takes his money,
everybody else looks down,
and the man with a stereo
hanging from his throat
like a horse's feedbag, when he goes,
he takes the music with him.

The Shapeshifting Secret Agent Gets Caught Discarding A Sweater Knitted By His Girlfriend

Honey, you have to understand:
I was the book that became
the dart that flew clean through
the desert warlord's throat. I was a house
fly riding into the mansion on
the coattails of the Russian ambassador.
I've been a French maid with
a malfunctioning bodice, a dolphin
trailing the dictator's yacht,
the butler whose wrinkled fists could
make paste out of petrified walnuts.
In all cases, truly, I am as naked
as my profession requires.
What you see as a kilt
or a tastful pantsuit is just my skin,
as open-minded as stem cells.
Otherwise, I'd find myself tangled
halfway between taxi driver and prostitute,
trying to shrug off a tuxedo or a ball-
room gown suddenly twice my size
as some vengeful sniper closed one eye.
Listen, I know you mean well but
this yarn might as well be the fishing net
that nearly drowned me once
until I remembered I could change
into water. Besides, doesn't it
look like I'm already wearing it, even now?
Don't you think I heard you lying
right next to me in your separate gown,
your long needles clicking in the dark?

The Dying Breed

I donned a dark blue tank-top on my way
to the Trump protest because nothing
shuts down a loudmouth bigot like nineteen
inch arms, but before I could
cross over to the left side of the street,
a gliding fellow in eyeliner called me
a Neanderthal, then this potbellied guy
in a trucker hat asked if I meant to
knock that first guy on his ass and if so
I'd better wear gloves because of *the AIDS*,
then Trucker Hat looked confused
when I went to stand with the throng
of rail-thin college kids peppered
with black drag queens, and the whole
time Eyeliner Guy kept looking over at me
like I was some kind of Manchurian protester,
and even amidst all that noise and naked
Germanic rage, I just kept thinking
about how the TV told me that Neanderthals
invented the flutes from the bones
of dead songbirds then died
out so that homo sapiens had to
invent flutes all over again, bamboo
piccolos sailing westward from Byzantium,
migrating from the woods of nameless hunters
to the concern halls of Italy and France,
no longer bone-carved but steel,
capable of bending one shrill breath
into more notes than some can hear
let alone have the good sense to applaud.

The Man with Six Hands

may not have seen
the face of God
but he made a wicked
swimmer, so many
chlorinated molecules passing
between his fingers
that he blurred
towards the finish line
where a blue-
eyed sweetheart
with brothers in the war
smiled and knelt as
she held the towel open.

The Animal Morgue

I'm sure there are more depressing places—
say, a day-long tour of Auschwitz—
but surely, room must be made on the list
for the veterinarian leading us back to collect
the remains of Lieutenant Fuzz
from one of a half-dozen stainless steel
drawers shut along the wall of this
refurbished kitchen, so that as we take turns
cradling her, it's almost like the morning
we opened the dresser to find her
fast asleep on my work slacks, unfazed
by however long she'd been trapped
in mahogany darkness, merely stretching
like a lyre washed in bedroom light
before sprinting away to hunt her fill.

The First Law of Thermodynamics

Dig too far and you'll find the shards
of something ancient, stacked like Rome
and San Francisco on the crust
of ancestors: streets capping ruins,
ziggurat plus bazaar equals taco stand.
Sooner or later, all the cloisters
in your abbey become eligible
for an upgrade. All you have to do
is peel back your bedroom wallpaper
and you'll find a whole tiramisu
of lost history. Remember, atoms are
just bags of cowbells—electrons, leptons,
quarks, the mayfly's sparkler lifespan.
How many cowbells in a tulip,
a woolly rhino, a taxidermist, cowbells
sloughing through the pastures
of Tel Aviv, tin song that used to be
my mother now recycling that anthem
of hay and flies and runaway sun.

Why Don't You Dry Off After You Shower?

asked the pretty blonde in my dorm
the semester I almost hung myself
from the stairwell with an extension cord,
partly because of a dead mother
and a weak bladder, still years before
a masked woman dipped a scalpel in the dark,
but mostly because I wasn't getting laid.
I don't remember what I told her,
though I suspect I simply liked the appearance
of sauntering in from the rain,
a little wild-eyed, friendless
but perfectly fine, like the Zen monks
I'd read about, and not another lonesome kid
obsessed with the thickness of his biceps.
Which reminds me of an afternoon
walking back from a physics lecture
when the clouds opened up and everybody
but me ran—everybody but me and this
plain-faced girl walking the other way,
her hair like tarnished gold,
both of us smiling as we passed
each other, too afraid to say hello.

Stoplight

It's terrible
to be caught yelling
at your crotch
next to a minivan
full of kids
and a young mom
just pulling out
of the parking lot
of Ambassador Baptist,
no still soft voice
informing them about
the cell phone
you just dropped
on your lap,
let alone the call
that won't go
through to
the hospice ward
in which your grand-
father wants
to say goodbye
to the only
member
of the family
who didn't inherit
his temper.

Patriotic Cookie

The sign says it only costs a dollar,
either because of or in spite of
the poorly melted frosting, tri-colored
palette of sprinkles smeared by California heat
into a kind of murky blue not half
as impressive as the brighter hue adorning
the tiles on the Islamic mosque
I just saw in a documentary
about some desert with apostrophes,
and still less impressive when
compared to the adjacent seafood aisle
with its plucky crab legs and shy
grammatical shrimp, canned goods
with their Depression-era robustness,
roasted chickens in their bodices of spice,
all those exhibitionist heaps of melons
and well-marbled steaks, and of course
the wall-to-wall display of diapers
which do their best to whitewash
the horror that happens down below.

Flight Safety Instructions

In the event of a water landing,
this poem will not save you.
That's because words cannot be used
as flotation devices anymore
than they can replace good
old-fashioned adult supervision
during a rousing game of lawn darts.
Also, be advised that talking
like this means we've broken down
the fourth wall though such walls
are only made of air anyway,
meaning that under just the right
conditions they like anything can be
squeezed down into a star.
It could be that I've failed to grasp
the intricacies of nuclear fusion
but there's still this poem
on your end and this laminated
placard on mine, vibrating in its sheathe
sewn to the ass-end of somebody
else's chair, and as the plane
banks between mountains
hemmed in by vast deep lakes,
I take it out and study the family
depicted as white and unafraid,
merely bending as though in prayer,
as though whispering to God hey
God what did we do to deserve this?

Maybe

the girl rolling her eyes
as she waits in line
beside her mother
at Victoria's Secret
isn't thinking
that the world is hers
so much as it's not
her mother's anymore
than it's mine
and why should she
waste time listening
to the ones who
never broke out
of whatever kept them
zipped inside their skins
like the mice
in the snake's belly
with their teeth
and their smartphones
and all those friends
they forgot
long before their own
firstborn needed
braces or a co-signer
and something old
to put her back against.

Part Time Job

I almost got my eyes burned out
one Saturday afternoon back in Iowa
when a chicken broaster
exhaled a plume of boiling-hot grease
that, somehow, landed perfectly
on the glasses I almost never wore.
I'd like to say I stopped
pining after the girls waiting tables
for long enough to imagine life
without these nubs of glorified gelatin,
but honestly, who does that?
A clothesline separated the kitchen
from the room where girls with eyeliner
and no bodyfat made ice cream cones,
and pinned to that line were all
the orders I had to fill before
the boss would let me go home
with a quart of whatever was left over
to keep me company in my russet Ford
while gnats danced in the streetlights,
porch swings creaked like thuribles
and kids rode by on bicycles, laughing.

The Next Generation of Poets

In another dimension
all our poets are gathering
along that kidskin border
where our country bleeds
into Mexico. They've brought
what look at first like bricks,
white bricks that take
two hands to carry—but no,
they're unpublished
manuscripts. One by one,
they stack them up
while the National Guard
does their best to block
the wind. When they're done,
a tangerine-faced
Donald Trump gives
a speech that has nothing
to do with poetry. Later,
once everyone else has gone,
hungry families arrive
and start climbing the wall
or simply push through,
except for those few
who ignore the rumbling
of bellies and guns and stop
to thumb through fallen pages.

The Lowest Wall in Human History

Though it stretches for thousands
of miles, across deserts and mountains
and the bright snakeskin of rivers,
it's almost impossible to see,
dwarfed by the thickness
of a baby's fingernail, no more
than a molecular smear of granite.
They say the builders needed
tweezers and microscopes
as they stooped like rice-planters.
In fact, the wall's so low that we might
be standing on it right now.
We might even be part of it.
And to think, we never felt a thing.

III.

The Great Speech

When the dictator began shouting
and gesturing, the children ran
back behind the crowds, where a cracked

and overturned tank had filled
with rainwater in which the children
could swim. Why don't

our parents play like this?
one asked, stretching beneath the stars.
The others shook their heads.

When I Was a Kid, So Many Died

by blundering into pits of quicksand
that I half-expected to sink every time
I navigated my stubby legs

through a hospital parking lot,
a blind alley, a playground after rain
made mud roil off the biblical deep.

And that universal lesson imparted
by so many TV shows: *Don't
struggle*, requiring a kind of

Zen-like acceptance of our fate,
the grim knowledge that if it struck,
when it struck, we were fucked

unless a friend was passing by
with a rope coiled over one shoulder,
or a tree branch just happened

to be hanging low enough that it
could be grasped, and bent,
and climbed like a tether to the sky.

On The History Channel's Lack Of Imagination

I like the idea of parallel dimensions
if only so that I can get a medal
for beating the crap out of anyone who believes

in ancient aliens—as though our ancestors
were too dense to move a statue
or jigsaw limestone into a skyscraper,

like we're living in the only time it's possible
to turn over a bucket and dream
of a helmet with an umbilical cord.

Machismo

I have to admit, I laughed
when the guy who said he'd been
studying taekwondo

for so long that he could
kill a man just by touching him
got knocked out in a bar

not by a punch but a YIELD sign
pulled off the wall
by the band and thrown

into the audience like a Frisbee
or a flying guillotine
skimming over beer steins

that he didn't block because
*A real man never raises his hand
unless he's ready to kill.*

Jack Dreams Of Attics And Snowfall

Jack has never met anybody named *Jack* before,
except in bad action movies and the romance novels
his mother used to read, which Jack read too

for the sex scenes because he was home-schooled
and bereft of lessons on female anatomy.
Jack's father died in the war, in an airport bathroom,

in a train explosion. Hard to say. But sometimes,
Jack pretends he's alive and comes back
to get him, and isn't at all perturbed that Jack

has grown pudgy in spite of his barbed wire tattoo.
We all do things we regret. Jack's mother
taught him that. One time, Jack watched a race

on television, a runner so damn fast he almost
lapped his opponents. Jack noticed that by the end,
it looked just like the winner was in last place.

Not-God, Standing on the Beach, Talking to Herself

What's across the ocean

                                        Listen,

is just other people wondering

                                        what rots only rots

what's across the ocean

                                        because it can't last forever.

Ode to the Getaway

Last night, I broke my brother out of jail
using Tommy guns and a tandem bike.
Granted, he didn't look much like me

what with his immaculate white suit and cigar,
his blurred face, his accent that kept
shifting from Chicagoan to Samoan

with just a dash of Welsh-Irish thrown in,
but that's just what happens after whiskey
and hot wings and a few hours' sleep.

Besides, when I finally felt up to leaving
my bed, then the house, I passed a stranger
who might have been my real brother's twin

right down to the goatee and hairline,
plus those jaywalking Bohemian eyes
as he shouldered by, The Times in hand,

coffee spilling down his shirt-sleeve
so that for a moment it resembled gun oil
left over from our daring border break.

So that I nearly stopped him, this stranger,
and asked where he'd been all this time,
and most of all, if he still remembered

the cops with their curses and sirens
and Prohibition mustaches falling
further and further behind our ludicrous bike

as we made for that seaside village
where surely pretty girls waited
under dark trees heavy with foreign fruit.

The Man Who Rises

He goes out after midnight
and lifts fire to his mouth
so that the wispy smoke escaping

his back porch resembles
the looping orbits of the planets
not just around our sun but through

the whole Milky Way, an arm
of which he sees as he glances up
in silence, practically a model

for Zen contemplation
were it not for the carcinogens,
the plants in need of water,

the frayed bathrobe
and the dog pawing the screen,
softly whining to get out.

Eighth Grade

My family's idea of a vacation
was staying at the Lamplighter Motel
two towns over, forty bucks

for temporary access to cable
and a swimming pool,
which I usually avoided because

I didn't want anyone to see
my calves, those broken flippers,
but one time I got talked into trunks

and just kind of walked around
waist-deep in the musk of chlorine,
thinking this wasn't so bad,

maybe it was time I taught myself
to do more. So I let the water
slip past my neck, kicked

like a dying lobster, moved
only half a foot toward the ladder.
Still, my heart soared

until I straightened up
and saw some drunk bastard
snickering from the upstairs bar,

waving for me to join him.
I'd never seen him before
but I can still see his hayseed cap,

that familiar locker room smirk,
and most of all, the fact
that my parents sat two tables

away from him, and they were
looking down at me too,
and they were also laughing.

Algebra Taught Me Nothing

plus nothing equals more
Nothing. Still,
When winter paws

the windows, our limbs
by some instinct
older than

words know
to press, to tangle
like a celtic knot, fractals

of dark matter,
both shivering yet warm
to the other's touch.

My Mother's Left Eye

After "Grace" by Eric Enstrom

I don't know why I remember that painting
hung over mashed potatoes at the Gingham Inn,
a dreary Russian-looking fellow praying

over bread near real tables where farmers lifted coffee
in the ceramic clatter of their daily rest.
Maybe it has something to do with my mother

who was reading the cafe's newspaper
one afternoon when I dove for the comics,
pulled those colors from the folds and somehow

left a papercut across her left eye.
So that for days after, she wore an eye patch
that wasn't nearly as cool as the ones

on TV though she assured everyone
it wasn't my fault, all of this joined somehow
in the Proustian soup of my brain

to a drab old man leaning over golden fists
of bread, his famous arch of piety and forgiveness:
two things that have always made me wince.

Dear Jung

It's not that I'm afraid
of burning houses or broken
teeth or the breasts

of my long dead mother.
Rather, I'm awake now,
the window's open

from last night
and a woman I love
just brought me strong coffee.

Besides, I know
they'll all still be there
whenever I get

around to them,
waiting with the patience
of wet stones.

Written at an Outdoor Café After News of Another American Killed in Battle at Afghanistan

While a nearby couple discusses Jane Austen,
men across the street are tearing the room off a house.
Shingles fall like one-winged butterflies,

or maybe moths—the ones that change their color
after a couple generations of roosting near factories.
It's a day for frozen yogurt and iced coffee

sweating in rings but these workmen in ball caps
and knee pads go on, stooped like oil derricks--
even the new guys tethered like fetuses

to the steeples—hammering and hammering.
Except for when a breeze ghosts over the lot—
nothing miraculous, just a knot of air

cresting the tops of cars, the plumage of trees,
these men just high and smart enough to pause,
turn, and mouth it with their sunburnt faces.

On the Matter of Syrian Refugees, or Poem Written In The Seventy-Eight Year In Which We Haven't Learned A Thing

They came to escape the busted glass,
the children with broken noses,
those looming smiles bound up in kinked crosses,

about a thousand souls clutching the rails
of an ocean liner named after a city
known for birthing jazz, which stopped

first at Cuba, then the US., then Canada,
turned away each time in the name
of prudence, so sorry, there's just not enough

time for that kind of extreme vetting.
Imagine the long trip home, how every breeze
twisted like a knife made of bone.

How shame and fear inhabit the same side
of the same silver coin. It should be
remembered that off the coast of Florida,

that crowded death-ship found itself

surrounded not by stern men with pencils,
let alone Christians with blankets,

but American gunships—a goddamn swarm
sent to make sure nobody swam for it.
I'll not say these were your parents,

your young, for the dead are just dead.
But I think that you and I are floating on a raft
that is actually a great door

torn off its hinges, and there's an arm
rising out of the fog, holding aloft a torch
that might glow if it weren't made of stone.

Upon Hearing that the Ringling Brothers Circus Is Closing Down After 146 Years

It all starts with jugglers, usually
immigrants with elaborate mustaches
touring town halls to the applause

of farmers who can only look
at fallow fields so long without crying.
In time, a horse and a dancing bear

get involved, then women on trapeze,
elephants like blunted scimitars.
Boys sell paper bags soaked in butter.

Tents thicken, a little bit related
to blouses. Meanwhile, those farmers
go off to war and come back,

or not. Teir children grow tall
then stoop and wither, biplanes

transform into jets that bleed
across the clouds like eyeliner.
So much becomes beautiful

on retrospect, including the whip
and the tiger that bows in spite
of fur that knows no rhyme.

How to Be a Good Buddhist

It's not about appreciating
simple moments. In fact, you shouldn't
until long after they've passed,

and all at once for no reason
you feel this nearly
unendurable affection for

the sunlight slanting
somebody's backyard near a grill
and a cooler full of beer,

or the way she gathered up
her hair as she stood in the shower,
not yet out of love with you,

or the child now grown
leaning over sofa to pet a dog
whose name you don't remember.

Too Late

I should have got myself
enlightened on some hilltop
between daffodils

and pastures of horseshit,
stopped fucking,
stopped eating meat,

gave up liquor, maybe
even taught at some monastery
where I knelt straight

as a sixpenny nail
for hours, always smiling
at the mice behind the walls,

then when I finally felt
my chest unknotting
stunned everyone

by ordering a hooker,
an alarmingly rare steak,
a fat glass of Scotch

that tastes like rainwater
shushed through the arms
of fire-hardened trees.

Ode to Nothingness

A caveman dressed in reindeer leather
whittles a flute from the wing of a vulture
and four hundred centuries later,

not one of us knows the tune he played
as he limped across prehistoric France,
not especially concerned with what

we might call the *soul* of that vulture,
its immutable cinder—just that the breeze
felt good on his face and isn't it lovely

how breath makes sound, how rocks
yield fire and even dung grows flowers,
how the earth makes music of our bones?

About the Author

Michael Meyerhofer's debut poetry book, *Leaving Iowa,* won the Liam Rector First Book Award. His third, *Damnatio Memoriae* (lit. "damned memory") won the Brick Road Poetry Book Prize. He has also been the recipient of the James Wright Poetry Award, the Annie Finch Prize for Poetry, and other honors, including five chapbook prizes. Since 2011, he has served as the Poetry Editor of *Atticus Review.* His own poems and stories have appeared in *Ploughshares, Rattle, North American Review, Hayden's Ferry, Asimov's Science Fiction Magazine,* and other journals. In addition to poetry, he has published a fantasy series. For more information and an embarrassing childhood photo, visit <u>troublewithhammers.com</u>.

Glass Lyre Press

exceptional works to replenish the spirit

Glass Lyre Press is an independent literary publisher interested in technically accomplished, stylistically distinct, and original work. Glass Lyre seeks diverse writers that possess a dynamic aesthetic and an ability to emotionally and intellectually engage a wide audience of readers.

Glass Lyre's vision is to connect the world through language and art. We hope to expand the scope of poetry and short fiction for the general reader through exceptionally well-written books, which evoke emotion, provide insight, and resonate with the human spirit.

Poetry Collections
Poetry Chapbooks
Select Short & Flash Fiction
Anthologies

www.GlassLyrePress.com

www.ingramcontent.com/pod-product-compliance
Lightning Source LLC
Chambersburg PA
CBHW020145130526
44591CB00030B/236